The Writings On The Wall

EILEEN DISTASIO-CLARK

Copyright © 2024

All Rights Reserved

With Great Love and Appreciation to Those Who Have and Do Bless My Life.

My Family:

Joseph DeStasio Sr. & Miriam Lucille Baragone DeStasio, My Late Parents.

Andrea Jean DeStasio McIntosh, My Older Sister and Their Families.

Joseph DeStasio Jr., My Younger and Only Brother and Their Families.

Donna Marie DeStasio Wagner, My Younger Sister and Their Families.

My Children:

Eileen, Rebekah, Rachel, S. Michael,

Jennifer, Sharon, Tara, Stephanie,

Apryll, Mikaelah, & M. Trevor

and THEIR Families!!

ACKNOWLEDGMENTS

First and foremost, I express, deeply, my sincere gratitude to our Heavenly Father for blessing me with the gift and talent of writing! I know I could not do what I do without His assistance. I also want to thank Him for the inspirations I and my children received that brought about many of these Thoughts and Sayings!

And, of course, I thank my children, Eileen, Rebekah, Rachel, S. Michael, Jennifer, Sharon, Tara, Stephanie, Apryll, Mikaelah, and M. Trevor for the contributions they made both in creating and receiving these thoughts.

CONTENTS

INTRODUCTION

I am a mother of eleven wonderful children! As a mother, because I love being a mother and I dearly love all of my children, children-in-law, and grandchildren, I have always wanted to do all that I could to provide the best learning and growth, the most secure development of relationships and self-images. I have always wanted to do all I could for their best good!

Ergo, one of the things I did was create thoughts that I thought were thought-provoking and would help them feel better, do better, and be better. So that everyone would be able to see them, I wrote them on the wall that surrounded the bathtub and sometimes, on the mirror above the bathroom sink.

I created many of these thoughts, which are compiled in the first section of this collection. However, some of them arose in conversations with my children. Those thoughts are compiled in the second section of this collection. Others were the notes I wrote in the margins of my Scriptures when I was doing my Scripture Study. Those notes are compiled in the third section of this collection.

THE WRITING ON THE WALL: MY THOUGHTS

1. I cannot be defeated by anyone nor anything because I will not be defeated by the only one who could defeat me, me! And I WILL NOT defeat myself!
   (My personal motto.)
2. Remember who you are, where HOME is, and how to get there!
   Choose the Right! Hold to the Rod! Return with Honor! (My family motto.)
   [Note: The final three phrases are from teachings of The Church of Jesus Christ of Latter-Day Saints.]
3. If you are early, you are on time,
   If you are on time, you are late,
   If you are late, you are rude! (My advice to…)
4. It does not matter what others think of you; what matters is what Heavenly Father thinks of you. (My memory, in words, of what Sister Theresa said to me, when I was a child.)
5. Every day is a good day, if you make it that way.
6. Smile! If you smile, you will think you are happy. If you think you are happy, you will feel happy. If

you feel happy, you will be happy. If you are happy, you will smile. So, smile, even in the morning!

7. If Heavenly Father says, "No," do not ask, "Why," ask, "Then what instead."

8. If *he* says, "Go and do," you may ask, "Why."
   If He says, "Go and do," just say, "Ok."
   Because when *he* speaks, you may question man's wisdom.
   But when He speaks, you can trust in God implicitly!
   So, when "Go and Do" is the Lord's message to you, reply quickly, "Anything for Thee."

9. Do not put off for tomorrow what you can at least begin today, or something may arise to take that opportunity away.

10. Live as if you are poor. Give as if you are rich!

11. Desire is the force that motivates us to achieve our goals. Faith is the power that compels us to believe that we can.

12. Keep your commitments the way you agreed to them.

13. Potential is always and only potential unless and until it meets action, commitment of mind, and sincerity of heart. Then it becomes a reality.

14. Because you usually get what you work for!

Reach for the stars and you may glow; shoot for the moon and you could shine; aim for the sun and you will radiate!

15. Once upon a time... there was a time... when there was time.

16. Hope, when given credence, becomes:
Belief, which, when fed by action becomes,
Faith, which, when coupled with good works becomes,
Knowledge, which, when internalized inspires,
Charity, which never faileth.

17. The difference between bad people and good people is marked by the pitchfork or the steeple. The difference between good people and great people is seen in the way they treat people.

18. No one should be completely independent from everyone. But everyone, in as much as possible, should be self-reliant, and totally dependent on no one.

19. Another day, another dollar? No, no, it is more like pennies. Oh well, rather pennies than pebbles.

20. To look is not to see. Seeing just happens. You have to choose to look, sometimes more intently, sometimes away.

21. Humility is the art of knowing that there is more to you than "you," that more than you made "you," that even when you are great, "you" are

nothing and when you are nothing, "you" are great. Ergo, humility is the realistic balance of perception between believing you are nothing and thinking you are the world.

22. Reason, is the "why" for what you do.
Excuse, is a shift of blame to anyone but you.

23. Fair does not mean you get what everyone else gets; it means you get what is best for you.

24. You cannot be pulled into the world without first letting go of the Lord.

25. If you do not like the truth about yourself, Change It, by changing yourself.
But remember to make those changes in an eternally upward direction.

26. Whether they are good or bad, habits are easier to make than to break; so, do it right the first time.

27. You might as well be the kind of friend you want to have because you will have the kind of friends others see you be.

28. It feels good to feel good, and that is how you feel when you do good. So, do good!

29. In all ways on all days, be the very best you that you can be. Heavenly Father asks no more than that, and He expects NO less!

30. You can be peaceful without being passive, a fighter without being an aggressor. By being a **D**efender and not an **O**ffender.

31. Relationships do not just work. You have to work to make them work.

32. A universally appropriate prayer:
Help me be what I need to be, to be like Thee, so I can be with Thee, Eternally!

33. Whether we follow Heavenly Father's directives or complain against them and refuse them, depends upon our faith and focus.

34. Where there is a difference of perspective, the efforts that fail are applied to man's ideas; those that succeed are applied to God's!

35. Home is where my heart is. Where is yours?

36. It is not unidirectional... So, Respect and Expect Respect!

37. Evolution, the perfect study to pursue if you want to do one of two things:
- Exhibit justifiable anger.
  Or
- Practice anger management skills.

38. My ideas are good,
Sometimes they are even great,
But Heavenly Father's ideas are always better;
That is why they are worth the wait.

39. Despite your life's experiences or because of them, you can be a great success or a total failure, the choice is yours.

40. Put life into your life by living it with a worthy purpose, deep commitment, and trust in God.

41. Emotion is not a strong reason for commitment. It is often of the moment and therefore, inspires only motivation for the moment.

42. Those who truly love you do not love you because they are supposed to; they love you because they do.

43. If "all you want to do" is what you do for you, then anything you do for anyone else will seem like everything, and too much because you would rather do less.

But...

If "all you want to do" is what you can do for others, then everything you do for everyone will seem like nothing or not enough because you will want to do more.

44. When all is said and done, all that was said and done will be all that can be said and done. So, say and do what is right while you still can.

45. The choice always remains with you, regardless of the nature, strength, or source of the influence, for good or for bad.

46. We must believe before we can receive.

47. Life can be good, if you do what you should, and not seek what you would, if you could.

48. It is one thing when a person **cannot** help; it is quite another thing when a person ***will not*** help.

49. When you help where help is not needed, you cannot expect that help to meet the need. So first, identify the need.

50. Do you really know; do you just believe; or do you only hope?

51. Just as it requires study and effort to learn an academic subject, skill, or talent, work is required for spiritual growth and learning. It will come no other way.

52. One who is out of harmony with Heavenly Father's laws, cannot be in tune with His spirit.

53. Things are today what they need to be, so they can be tomorrow what they should be.

54. The anticipation of fear is frightening.

55. You will never be more than what you are if nothing more is expected of you.

56. If Heavenly Father expects you to do more, it is because you can! (Inspired by an answer to a prayer.)

57. You did not do anything you did not do!

58. Making a bad day good is an achievement. Making a good day bad is a failure.

59. You have heard that less is more, but better is not best!
No, he who makes the most of his days is the one who most greatly enjoys his rest.

60. If you want Heavenly Father to do for you what you cannot do for yourself, you must first do all

that you can do, not only what you want to do, or
just what you *think* you can do, but ALL that you
actually can do. Then, He will do the rest.

61. Sometimes it is necessary to step back, or even
down, in order to move forward and climb higher.

62. It is easier to be alone when you are alone than
when you are in the company of others.

63. Perseverance without expectation usually leads
to pleasant rewards.

64. If you have to speed to not be late, leave earlier
or stay home.

65. Remember, because we are family, what you do
to your name, you do to mine.

66. The love of family equals the price of happiness.

67. The best person to be is the person you would be
if Jesus were your constant companion.

The best way to behave is the way you would
behave if our Heavenly Parents were with you
always.

The best way to speak is the way you would speak
if the Angels were recording your
communications.

The best reason to be that person, behave that
way, and speak like that is because Jesus and our
Heavenly Parents are with you, if you let Them
be, and the Angels do record—more than just
your words—your thoughts and actions too.

68. If you smile through your trials and sorrows, you will feel better, even before you or they get better.
69. The height of your greatness is only equal to the depth of your humility.
70. Mistakes may be made because of ignorance or weakness. Wrong choices are made with knowledge because of rebellion.
71. What do you like about your life right now, not as you dream it, but as you live it? Focus on that!
72. The more we learn, the more you will realize how little we really know!
73. If we are to become masters of ourselves, we must learn to master ourselves in any situation and under any circumstances.
74. A true exemplar is not one who tells you what you should do; it is one who is doing what you should do.
75. Your nighttime dreams are fed by your daytime thoughts. What do yours reveal?
76. Life is good, if you are.
77. Motivation born of desire is great indeed, but far stronger and more compelling is motivation born of need. So, from life, let us learn this lesson and remember to heed the motivation most likely to succeed, is the one fed by a desire that creates a need.
78. Different is not necessarily better or worse. Sometimes different is just different.

79. To receive no help when you have sought it makes you feel unimportant and unloved. To receive the help you sought suggests that you are both important and loved. To receive unsolicited help, not only tells you that you are important and loved, but that you are significant enough to be noticed.

Likewise...

To give no help when help is not sought, makes others feel unimportant and unloved. To give help when others seek it suggests that they are both important and loved. To give unsolicited help, not only tells others that they are important and loved, but that they are significant enough to be noticed.

Therefore, give without waiting to be asked.

80. It is good to invite! It also feels good to be invited! Since one must invite another to be invited, it is upon all of us to do the inviting, so everyone can be invited!

81. It is the trials of imperfection that enable us to become perfected.

82. Because it is natural to learn by imitation, there is nothing wrong with being a copycat, if you are copying a good cat!

83. Even those who consider themselves greater than others are but a bent knee before the Lord.

84. Be careful to not look beyond the mark, but strive to see deeper than the surface.

85. Sometimes, when we are searching for the obvious, we are inclined to look for more than we need to find.

86. You should always strive to be the person others know they can come to for help.

87. The Direction of Progression is up, not down, and forward, not backward.

88. Strive to be as perfect as you want others to believe you are.

89. If you want to improve your vision, look through the eyes of love.

90. No one is perfect; we all make mistakes. So, when you think or know you have "goofed," remember; the best remedy for a bad choice is a sincere apology.

91. There is always hope, and there is always help, if we are worthy to receive it and willing to see it.

92. What is most important is to appear to be what you truly are and to truly be what you appear that you are.

93. Council from the Lord will not always be easy to understand, but it will never be too hard to obey!

94. To dream is good. Setting goals is essential. But remember, we cannot find what we do not seek, and we cannot obtain what we do not work for.

95. When unrelenting burdens give place to self-doubt and cause you to question your worth, remember this; trials are sometimes the consequences of problems yet unsolved, and not the result of a rebellious soul, nor the product of inadequacy.

96. If you do not want to be put in your place, Stay IN Your Place!

97. Think before you speak or act, and consider this. The truth always, in its time, reveals itself.

98. Faith does not require understanding. It only demands that we place our trust in God.

99. If you throw away a soiled garment, it is gone forever. If you wash it, you can wear it again. Think about that when you err, and when others make mistakes.

100. If you want your children to learn intelligent speech, speak to them intelligently.

101. The freedom that God gave to us in the premortal world is the freedom to choose between right and wrong, not to make wrong right.

102. The competitive mind is not a rational mind, and the competitive heart is not a compassionate heart.

103. When it comes from God, counsel is as good as commandment!

104. Remember to remind yourself to remember.

105. Truly successful people do not have bad days. They just have days that enlighten their minds, soften their hearts, help them reach a little higher, and stand a little taller.

106. We could all do well to be like people of small stature, who look up to all others and down on no one!!

107. What are the things you loved most when you were too young to choose what you liked?
Those are the things you love most!

108. Challenge is the schoolmaster of life. Whether you pass or fail its coursework depends upon the direction of your perspective.

109. Money may pay the doctor's bills, but it is not a cure for the wound.

110. Do not just turn a blind eye to the darkness in others; choose your actions and reactions by who and what you are, not by what they do, say, or are.

111. Do your best to be your best, so we can all go home together.

112. Heavenly Father has ways of working things out, and His ways always work out!

113. True champions do not compete with others; they master themselves.

114. The influence of the Adversary hardens the heart and dulls the mind, but the Spirit of the Lord softens the heart and quickens the mind.

You are the one who chooses which influence you will follow.

115. Every strength can prove to be a weakness, and every weakness can serve as a strength.

116. The difference is determined by the state of the mind—optimistic or pessimistic, positive or negative, open or closed.

117. Giving up only lets you down, so DO NOT!

118. Two people walking on different paths, cannot arrive at the same destination!

119. Too much of anything good may cause us to boast of ourselves, and too little may cause us to feel abandoned.

120. Through trials, we grow! Times of trial are like school and times of joy are like the summer vacation, although sometimes they are only a spring break!

121. The righteousness of one cannot save another, and the wickedness of one cannot condemn the other.

122. In the end, we get what we gave along the way.

123. To teach the truth, you must first learn and live the truth.

124. There is no grey area. We either love the Lord, live His gospel, and do His will, or we do not.

125. To be forgiven, you must forgive.

126. Speak the truth, live the truth, be a representation of the truth, and you will teach the truth, simply by being yourself.

127. If you please the Lord, you will displease the adversary. If you please the adversary, you will displease the Lord.

128. Live the gospel always—in all ways—on all days.

129. Judgment is the Lord's; it is for us to forgive.

130. Give graciously; receive gratefully.

131. To do good is to be good, and to be good is to do good.

132. Put on the Whole Armor of God and choose friends who are likewise clad. Also remember, only you can dress yourself!

133. We should be the example we would follow when seeking to know what Christ-like looks like.

134. Seek not to change the gospel to fit yourself; seek to change yourself to fit the gospel.

135. Learn to measure yourself by worthwhile measurements.

136. You cannot trounce someone you love or love someone you trounce, so do not compete!

137. The best leaders are teachers, and the best teachers are leaders.

138. If you lead from behind, you can both direct and support.

139. Trials are a necessary step in the upward climb of HOME. Everyone has them because everyone needs them, but we must remember that while different people's trials may be the same, their trials may be different!

140. Communication is the foundation for a successful relationship!

141. Does your burden feel greater than your strength? Trust God because if you could not handle it, you would not have it.

142. People are sometimes slow to change and even slower to accept something new, until they have lost the old.

143. When life goes wrong and people go astray, it may not always mean that they are following Satan, but it does mean that they are not following the Savior!

144. You have to be a strong person going in, or you will be a broken person coming out. But, if you are a strong person going in, you will be a stronger person coming out.

145. We are as we behave, and we behave as we think!

146. Before we can do it, we have to think about it, but how we think it depends upon how we have experienced it.

147. You can be schooled without a school, but you cannot be taught without a teacher.

148. Do you read the writing between the lines, or do you write it?

149. What did you want to do when you were too young to know what you wanted to do?

150. That is what you really want to do.

151. You never can find what you do not look for.

152. Offense cannot be given, if offense is not taken.

153. Expect enough from yourself to keep progressing, but do not expect so much that you think you have failed when you have only fallen.

154. A person who is forever given a hand out will forever put his hand out.

155. Look for the good, but see the reality.

156. If you think you are perfect, you never will be.

157. You cannot recall what you never knew.

158. If you do what Heavenly Father shows you that you need to do, you will be prepared to do what you said you would do, and you will be prepared in the right way and at the right time.

159. Live up to what you want to be, or admit what you are not.

160. The more one is allowed to get away with, the more one will push the limits.

161. The past is never the past as long as it is affecting the present.

162. We are constrained to be in the world; we are commanded not to be part of it.

163. You can do better because you know better because you are better.
164. We are so foolish to believe that we are not children anymore just because we are grown up.
165. Miracles happen in the lives of those who believe in God and in the lives of those who do not… not because of all they forgot but because of the little they remember.
166. It is not just about being right or wrong; it is also about being better or best. That is why there is only one prison of darkness, but there are three kingdoms of light.
167. Whatever we were given to do will be given to someone else to do, if we are not prepared to do it when it is time for it to be done! So, prepare yourself now to be prepared then.
168. It is easy to speak the words, but it is not always easy to experience the experience.
There, you chose the light

Now, do what is right.

Strive with all you might.
To avoid eternal night.
169. When you were THERE, you chose to come HERE, because you wanted to be THERE!
170. He did what He did because He wanted to do what was needed for me and needed for you to be able to go HOME and live there with Him too!

171. Do you ask, "What can I do for you?"
Or do you wait for the plea?
"Will you please help me?"
Do you live to love your Dearest Friend?
Or wait to receive the lift.
Of that Loving gift?

172. Obtain all the learning you can from **good** books and **good** people. Knowledge enriches your life. But to obtain the light of understanding, you need to possess Truth! The Facts of Man are often discovered to be Fiction. But God's Truths are Eternal and never fail.

173. How can you help uplift anyone if you avoid everyone?

174. The world is out of step with God's Kingdom. So, if you are in step with the world, you are out of step and not walking with the Lord!

175. It is not rational to think that competition and the gospel can coexist. The gospel is compassionate and all about loving people. Competition is merciless and all about beating people.

176. What you believe you cannot do, you will not do.

177. It is said by many that the good life is marked by comforts and pleasures. But those who have honestly looked have seen that the truly good life is adorned with sacrifice, service, and eternal blessings!

178. The experiences that drive us to the need for a Priesthood Blessing are blessings themselves because it is through life's trials that we can learn and grow!

179. Sometimes we need big trials to accomplish little changes that lead to huge accomplishments and humble triumphs.

180. When you think you have more troubles than you can bear, remember this: The Lord will <u>never</u> give you more than you can manage, but He will give you **all** that you can manage. So, know that you can and then get up and do, remembering always that the right choice is up to you!

181. When we understand that Heavenly Father's directives lead us where **we** said we wanted to go and provide the way for us to receive what **we** chose to come here to get, we cannot but see that He asks of us very little, while rewarding us with very much.

182. Success requires no less than total commitment and no more than absolute effort!

183. Blessings will not come if you do not believe it because even if they did you would not see it.

184. We cannot expect to know someone we have not met. We can know about them from others, but we need to meet them, interact with them, and communicate personally with them, to truly

know them. That is also how we come to know, and not just know about Jesus, our Lord and Savior, our Brother and Friend.

185. This day is the first day of the rest of your life. Whether it leads to failure or achievement depends on your focus. Do you look back with regret and resignation or ahead with hope and determination? The choice is yours, and yours alone!

186. The process of making decisions is like the process of baking a cake. What you get out of it depends upon what you put into it. Greater effort, with the right ingredients, produces more excellent results.

187. You can never go back to what you left. You may return to the same place, but it will be different. You may go back to the same people, but they will have changed. So, to appreciate life to its fullest, you must learn to look for and love the new in the old.

188. Nothing that can be said about anything can always be said about everything.

189. Turn "I would if I could" into "I can, and I will!"

190. You are the primary benefactor of all that you do for good!

191. Because we need all the help we can get to get through this life; we must change our name to

the Lord's name, and our focus from mine to
Thine.

192. If you think there is nothing wrong with what
you are, it is time to consider what you are not.

193. Yesterday is what it was. Today may be what it
is! Tomorrow is what you make it!!

194. The competitive nature of education, as
expressed through standardized competitive
testing, is counter-productive to the ultimate
goal of true education.

195. The hardest thing you have to do is always the
most important thing that has to be done.

196. It is always difficult to see ourselves, as we
really are when we are not what we thought we
were.

197. Words cannot say what actions do not convey.

198. Our thoughts reveal and create who and what
we are; we must control them, not be controlled
by them.

199. Recognition of one's fault against us, coupled
with the excusing of our own resulting negative
behaviors or beliefs, is the blood of blame. It
must be shed for us to heal and to grow, and
that can be accomplished only through the
sacrifice of self-justification and the acceptance
of responsibility for our proper use of agency—
the ability to choose better over worse, and best
over better.

200. Too much stimulation leads to a lack of satisfaction. Simplify and you will magnify!

201. Knowing the truth is always better than believing a lie.

202. You cannot fail unless you give up.

203. Keep going and do not limit yourself to just what you know now.

204. Things are always easier when they are possible than they are when they are real.

205. We know we must all pass through trials in order to grow, be strengthened, and excel both temporally and spiritually, but let us always strive to be the blessing, not the trial, in the lives of others.

206. The biggest decisions we make are to follow the smallest councils.

207. If your pace must change, step it up, do not slip it down. It is always encouraging to move ahead. It is usually discouraging to fall behind!

208. That which is truly worth obtaining, cannot be won in this life. Here, we work to grow, learn, and receive—from God—what we need to return Home, but we are given only what we are ready to receive. Temporal acquisitions, regardless of their nature, are of no worth beyond the need they meet. In the end, we all die and leave everything behind.

209. Therefore, let us put our greatest efforts into acquiring those things that are of true eternal worth—the Spiritual Gifts of God.

210. Everything physical is spiritual.

211. The importance of the family can never be overestimated; it can only be understated.

212. My day is so full of *whatever*, that I cannot figure out *what* I am *ever* going to do to catch up with myself. (In an email to Trevor.)

213. I keep thinking, "Today, I will have everything in order once again." Then, I get to the end of the day and I hear myself say, "I was so busy getting nothing done that I am ending the day in the same way I began it!" (In an email to Trevor.)

214. The greatest testimony of Heavenly Father's love for us is most easily seen in what could be called the "smallest of blessings," the things He does for us that we do not really need done. (In a text chat with Rachel.)

215. It is evident that Heavenly Father is taking care of us when, somehow, even when there is no way for things to work out, they still do. That is one of the most beautiful ways we can know that Heavenly Father is with us, even when we think we are alone.

216. We must know the truth to live the truth.

217. I need all the help I can get from Heavenly Father, because on my own, I am not enough to meet the demands of my own life. (In an email to Trevor.)

218. The truest measure of true love is the degree to which you live your life in such a way as to qualify for eternal life with your family.

219. Since life is not realistic, my goals have to be!

220. Just because not everything "goes according to plan," and there are times when it seems that "nothing goes according to plan," that does not mean that life is not worth the effort it takes to make it worth living.

221. Knowing that we are here to learn what we need to learn, do what we need to do, and become what we need to become in order to obtain what WE chose to come here to get— Eternal Life with our Heavenly Parents—and knowing that we could obtain this no other way, makes all of life worth the living!

222. Knowing that the Adversary does not want us to have what he lost because of his rebellion, softens the blows of his contentions against us because we can take comfort in the knowledge that we must be good enough, better than we realize, to be worth his efforts against us. For to be an enemy to the adversary, is to be an ally with God!

223. I have survived and thrived because I have refused to be defeated.

224. Journals are important!!

225. If historians of the past, those who lived the history of today, had not kept records, if people of the past had not kept journals, what would we know about history today? What would we know about our ancestors or ourselves in relation to our ancestors?
 What would we know?

226. Today, we are the ones living the history of tomorrow. What will future generations know of their history if we do not write it?

227. Keep a journal or a collection of journals; leave a legacy for those of tomorrow; you may never know the value you add to their lives until the day all histories are revealed.

228. I am not different because I want to be; I am different because I choose to be.

229. To do that which is good in the sight of God is to be different in the eyes of the world.

230. When all is said and done, what I want to have said to me, by the Lord about what I have done is this: "Well done, thou good and faithful servant."

231. An unavoidable rule of FAMILY is growing up. But growing up never has to mean growing apart, and it never should!

232. For relationships to thrive, civility is requisite, as is problem resolution. Therefore, remember, keeping the peace through silence does not always solve the problem, so communicate—with love!

233. I will not give up! I will not give in! I will not walk out! I will not let Thee down!

234. If I never knew how bad the bad could feel, I would never know how good the good does feel!

235. We can make whatever choices we want to make, but we cannot choose whatever consequences we want to choose. Every choice we make comes with its own set of consequences.

236. It is so much easier to find the right person when you are the right person.

237. Learn from the past. Live in the present. Look to the future.

238. Success, even in the most impossible situations, is possible when one has faith, courage, confidence, and a just cause.

239. To fear the Lord is to fear to disobey His word. To love the Lord is to obey His word. To serve the Lord is to do good to all men.

240. Where there is accommodation instead of acculturation, there is a divided nation.

241. Recognize your weaknesses so you know what you have to work on, but focus on your

strengths so you know what you have to work with.

242. When you plan, Do! and Always follow through.

243. When you begin, Complete!
hen Never yourself, your self-defeat!

244. Even when an endeavor is not what you expected to pursue, it is usually an opportunity that can help you get to where you are going in your journey to where you want to be.

245. There is no destiny except the one we make.

246. When searching for the "right" person, look, do not hunt!

247. It is no more beneficial to take responsibility for things you are not responsible for than it is to take no responsibility for what you are responsible for!

248. The best way to help yourself is to focus your efforts on the needs of others.

249. True faith in God, exhibited when times are good, is not lost when times are bad.

250. If you want to receive what you came here to get, you must do what you said you would do. Accept, with a sincere heart, God's truth; Live, with full commitment and integrity, His gospel; Serve, with genuine love, compassion, and selflessness, His children; Repent, with deeply felt, honest to the core, because you love God, remorse.

251. That which is of the temporal world is temporary.

252. We cannot rightfully credit ourselves for what God helped us to do. Rather, we need to acknowledge His hand in our lives and give thanks where it is due.

253. God's will is always the best course of action!

254. The wisest use of what we have is that of doing God's work, not the intent to gain more wealth and possessions.

255. It is so important to know where we are going, if we ever expect to get there.

256. There is intrigue in diversity but not strength. Some diversity enables growth, but where there is too much diversity, there is a loss of identity and "power." What we need is more acculturation and far less accommodation. Strength is founded in unity. Diversity lays the foundation for division.

257. If you only look for what you want to find, you may never find what there is to be found! But in your search and endeavor, make it good! Retrieve only what is right, and of true value and eternal worth!

258. It is through faith that those things which cannot be done are done, when they are the right things to do.

259. The destination has to be a good place for the journey to be worth the walk.

260. Sometimes you have to sacrifice what is too important to you to give up in order to obtain what is most important for you to have.

261. Faith is more powerful than fact.

262. We are never alone, unless we choose to walk the wrong path.

263. While experience is the architect of perspective, it is perspective that defines the experience.

264. The "true meaning" of the words we speak is evidenced by and only as powerful as the works that attend them.

265. Sometimes, for some things, any time can be the right time. However, for many things, there is "A" right time! Sometimes you have to wait for the right time, and sometimes you have to make the right time. Either way, Heavenly Father can help you do that!

266. If you knew that your mother or father, your brother or sister, your grandfather or grandmother, or uncle or aunt or cousin, or... was going to die tonight or tomorrow, what would you do today that you are not doing, or what would you not be doing that you are doing?

That is what you should be doing, or not doing, now!

267. The Letter of the Law is a great place to start, but it is not a good place to stop.

268. There is much good that can be drawn from every trial we face, IF we are willing to look for the good that we can learn, the good that we can do, and the good that we can become!

269. Be it knowledge of self or others, it is best obtained by focusing on the inner-self, for when you look on the outside, you never see the inside, but when you look on the inside, you see both the inside and the outside.

270. There will always be protection from the wiles of men for God's employees—those who do the work of the Lord.

271. No commandment is too difficult to obey. As we do what we can, Heavenly Father will provide what we lack so as to enable us to obey with fullness.

272. Whatever the Lord commands is right!

273. Free Agency gives us the power to choose to follow Christ or Satan. Thereafter, the way is prescribed.

274. It never has been, it is not now, and it never will be OK to disobey God.

275. There is no time, place, or way in which it is OK to not be on the Lord's side.

276. In my dreams, it is a reality; in reality, it is my dream—something to live for, something to work for, something to pray for!!

277. Do all you can to take care of yourself. Then, do all you can to help others in need. But, do not stop there! When you have done all that you can do for yourself, but it has not been enough, let others help you too. Afterall, if no one let anyone help them, how could anyone help anyone?

278. Heavenly Father will never give to us more than we can bear, but He will also never give us less. For if, we were given more, we would not have what we need to succeed, but if we were given less, we would learn nothing more than we already know.

279. Heavenly Father will speak to us in many ways, but we must be prepared to hear Him.

280. Because we are all blessed with the Light of Christ, regardless of background or teaching, everyone knows the difference between right and wrong.

281. Faith, Courage, Confidence, and a Just Cause, accompanied by Obedience to God's Laws, Prayer, and Fasting, lead to Victory over Self and the adversary, Growth and Achievement, and Lofty Eternal Rewards.

282. In all things, we should be an example of righteousness and holiness. Not, in anything should we exemplify or demonstrate worldly principles, not in thoughts, speech, or behavior, not in dress, entertain-ment, or vocation, not in principle, ideal, or values, not in anything!

283. One of the purposes of mortality is to demonstrate that one will remain faithful and obedient under all circu-mstances!

284. To be an example we must stand out, and we will always stand out when we do not fit in!

285. When you have done your best, what you have done is good enough! If, to someone else, your best was not good enough, the fault does not lie within you.

286. When you have done all that you could do, and would have done what should have been done, if what was done was not enough and if there was more that could have been done, Heavenly Father holds you unaccountable for what others may deem not good enough. Therein, the fault lies with them for what they did or did not do in response to all that you could and did do!

287. To make the journey matter, you must have a good destination to which you are headed.

288. Anything that needs to be done can be done if you are willing to do what needs to be done.

289. Be the You, you told your Heavenly Parents you would be. Better yet... BE BETTER YET!!

290. Before you can become what you want to be, you have to be who you are, for that is the foundation upon which you are building. So..., How true are you to yourself? How honest with others are you about yourself?

What do you do when no one is there to see, that you would not do if they were? What do you not do when no one is there to see, that you would do if they were?

Whether others are or arc not there... Be You! And Become Better! On your way to being Your Best— according to God's Standards!!

291. We do what we do in order to get done what needs to be done!

292. We do not need to understand someone to love him or her, and to care for him or her. We just need to do the things that Jesus would do.

293. Truth is Eternal! It always existed; God did not create it. Truth is elemental! Intelligence is the Light of Truth.

294. Our Spirits were created by Heavenly Father and Heavenly Mother is the express image or form of Their physical bodies.

295. In the Pre-Earth World we were taught:

a.   Eternal Truths: Right from Wrong as defined by that which enables us to gain Celestial Glory and Exaltation.

b.   About Mortal Life: What a physical body would be like; what life, itself would be like.

c.   About The Plan of Salvation: Laws and Ordinances instituted by God, which, if obeyed, would enable us to become like Them, Our Heavenly Parents.

d.   Preparation for Mortal Life: We had to advance far enough spiritually before we could/would/be ready for mortality.

e.   How to Use Agency: It was given to us THERE!

296. We were able to advance as far as we close to so do, especially far enough to be ready for mortality. Some were chosen—those who advanced enough—to perform certain works in this life, and were prepared for them. We served in positions in "The Eternal Church." We were taught the Plan of Salvation and how to live it.

The Writing on the Wall:
IN CONVERSATION WITH MY KIDS

In Conversation with **Eileen**:

298. No one, except God, is qualified to judge others. So, DO NOT!!

In Conversation with **Rebekah**:

299. We are not meant to fit into this world; we are meant to make ourselves fit for the

300. Kingdom of God. We must do that here, if we are to be able to go there.

In Conversation with **Rachel**:

301. We radiate what we are—good or bad!
302. When you engage in actions, it speaks loudly about what you are.
303. Definition of Multi-tasking = Making someone laugh while you are crying.

304. I want red and yellow ballet slippers, wrapped up in a "twash" bag, delivered by Mama La Poopa, over the railroad tracks, with a screw.

In Conversation with **S. Michael**:

305. You may not be cheerful about a challenge, but you can be cheerful through the challenge.
306. To be plucked out of secularism is the only way to be able to be nourished and flourished by God.
307. In a world where so many things are rushed through and not fully appreciated, we need to take the time to appreciate the small moments in between the big events.
308. Heavenly Father allows trials because He wants to strengthen us so we can stand. Satan causes them because he wants to weaken us so we will fall.
309. The greatest escape into fantasy is the one that fills you with the hope of a better reality.
310. It is in our weakest moments that we are made strong, if we do not give up, give in, or walk out.
311. We must go back in order to move forward. However, to get back, we must move forward, with the understanding that we can never return to what we left!

In Conversation with **Jennifer**:

312. Sometimes, the trial itself is a blessing.
313. I love how small this big world is!

In Conversation with **Sharon**:

314. In the face of too much diversity, simplicity is woven into complexity, and complexity becomes a mystery.
315. At different times, the same message may apply in different ways.

In Conversation with **Tara**:

316. When the offense is given, no reason is a good reason.

In Conversation with **Stephanie**:

317. The gospel is not true because it is mine; it is mine because it is true.

In Conversation with **Apryll**:

318. Just because I do not say things right, does not mean I am wrong.
319. I do not have time to deal with my life; I am too busy living it.

In Conversation with **Mikaelah**:

320. Same place, different space.

In Conversation with **M. Trevor**:

321. I do not give up on dreams; I change them.
322. We learn best how to spend money wisely after we have spent it foolishly.
323. What better time is there to get into shape than when you are out of shape?
324. A little bit here, and a little bit there, a little bit somewhere else, amounts to "That Much!"
325. To replace something useless or harmful with another form of the same thing is of no good to the body, mind, or soul.
326. Lift heavy, get big. Lift long, get strong.
327. You need to shower long enough and with cold enough water to cool me down!!
328. To punish one's worthy effort is to enable defeat.
329. They cannot stop caring just because you are not sharing.
330. You cannot go out to dinner with the Adversary and sit down to eat with the Lord, because they will not be at the same table, nor in the same diner.

The Writing on the Wall:

Margin Notes from My Scripture Studies

BIBLE—OLD TESTAMENT

Margin Notes from The First Book of Moses Called **Genesis**:

332. As he did with Eve, Satan uses partial truths to deceive with the intention of inducing disobedience. (2:4,5)

333. There are some things we just know, without teaching, but by The Light of Christ. (3:7)

334. Consequences are not always punishments. Punishments follow misdeeds, sins, and transgressions. Consequences follow choices; they may be good; they may be bad; it depends on the nature of the choice. (3:16-19)

335. Follow the example of the Savior and remain on the road to perfection, which continues beyond this life. (17:1)

336. Sometimes blessings do not come until it is obvious that they could only have come from God! (17:17)

337. The test of Abraham was a test of faith in the Integrity of God and involved the sacrifice of that which is most precious.
As with Abraham, any test of faith which we pass is followed by blessings!

338. The greater the test, when we pass it, the greater the blessings. (22:1-14)

339. Heavenly Father will speak to us with the number of times equal to the importance of the message. (41:32)

340. Heavenly Father can turn any circumstance in our lives into good. (50:20)

Margin Notes from The Second Book of Moses Called **Exodus**:

341. Restitution is closely linked to atonement, justice, and salvation. (23:2-7)

342. To the sincerely obedient, God promises guidance, protection, good health, defense against enemies, and inheritance in His Kingdom. (23:20,22,25-27,31)

343. A sacrifice is acceptable to God only when it is willingly made. A begrudgingly made sacrifice is a sin. (25:2)

344. There is one price for sin: repentance and repentance is the same for all. (30:15)

345. Because Heavenly Father gives us the opportunity to demonstrate what we will do for ourselves and others, we may, at times, be left to discuss courses of action with Him. By this, we can demonstrate our learning, growth, and progressions, or lack thereof.

(32:9-14)

Margin Notes from The Third Book of Moses Called **Leviticus**:

346. Sins committed unintentionally, by mistake, error, or oversight, still require proper and complete repentance. (4:2,3)
347. Hear, Act, Walk, According to the Commandments! (8:23,24)
348. Seek for the care and the good of others as you would seek for the care and good of yourself. (19:18)
349. Disobedience prohibits the Lord's blessings and presence in our lives. (26:23,24)

Margin Notes from The Fourth Book of Moses Called **Numbers**:

350. The Lord guides us generally. Many of the specifics must be chosen by us. (10:31,34)

351. When we follow the Lord, we are privy to His powers, but when His presence in our lives is denied, we lose His blessings. (14:9,22,23)
352. When we act without the Lord, we are not strong enough to win. (14:42)
353. Obedience is the simple solution. (21:8)
354. Those who are in favor with God cannot really be harmed by man. (23:8)
355. Sin cannot be hidden; it is rewarded for what it is. (32:23)

Margin Notes from The Fifth Book of Moses Called **Deuteronomy**:

356. Heavenly Father blesses the righteous and punishes the wicked. We choose the one we will be. (7:9,10)
357. The Lord provides and enhances our talents, but we must use them; we must do our part. (8:18)
358. Even just spending more time on other things and "only" getting around to prayer, scripture study, service, etc., is forgetting the Lord. (8:19)
359. We are to live the gospel exactly as God gave it to us. We do not leave anything out! We do not put anything in! No edits. No amendments. No rewrites. (12:32)

360. We have agency and the ability to make our own choices—right or wrong, good or bad. Therefore, no one is accountable for the sins of another; nor does one receive the blessings earned by another. (24:16)

Margin Notes from The Book of **Joshua**:

361. We must prepare, through proper inner cleansing, to receive the blessings and power of the Lord. (3:5)
362. Heavenly Father provides what and when we cannot. When we can, we must! (5:12)
363. Miracles are accomplished through the Laws of Nature, which are God's Laws. (6:20)
364. It is necessary to be willing and ready to remove evil from our midst. (22:12)
365. The Lord must come first, before everything else! (24:15)
366. Ultimately, our knowledge and testimony testify for or against us. (24:22)

Margin Notes from The Book of **Judges**:

367. When the young throw off their elders, they lose much in knowledge and guidance. (2:10)

368. It is typical of many people to believe that God
     has forsaken them, rather than acknowledge
     that they have forsaken God. (6:13)
369. That we may know the presence of God in our
     lives, He does for us only that which we cannot.
     (7:2)
370. Heavenly Father will sometimes provide
     assurance and guidance even when we do not
     seek it. He often provides those revelations
     through others. (7:10,11,13,14)
371. There is a limit to patience, but only through
     God can we know when the end of patience is
     reached. (10:11-13)
372. It is not our choices alone that affect us. Nor do
     our choices affect only us. (11:30-40)

Margin Notes from The Book of **Ruth**:

373. The Lord blesses us for both our faith and our
     loyalty. (2:12)

Margin Notes from The **First** Book of **Samuel**:

374. Parents are accountable, when they fail to
     teach their children correct principles and
     when they fail to correct their children when
     principles are violated. (3:13)

375. A sad truth; sometimes, some people treat others in ways they would not want others to treat them. (4:9)
376. The wicked fear the righteous because, though they may not know why, they sense the spirit of God abiding with the righteous. (18:12)
377. To behave wisely is to behave humbly, in a quiet manner, to be reverent, kind, long-suffering, to be responsible, dutiful, sacrificing, forgiving and penitent, to follow God and to strive to be like Christ at all times, on all days, and in all ways. (18:30)
378. The truly innocent need not argue their own defense; they can turn it over to God! (24:12,15)

Margin Notes from The **Second** Book of **Samuel**:

379. Punishment for unforgivable or unrepented sins may not come immediately, but it will come. (12:13)

Margin Notes from The **First** Book of **Kings**:

380. God will reveal His will for you, to you. (13:15-24)
381. We must put the Lord first in all things. (17:13,14)

382. The wicked and sinful blame others for their misfortunes, but it is their own choices which cause them trouble. (18:17,18)
383. Do not boast of a deed before it is done. (20:11)
384. The Lord does reward the repentant, but He can restore only what is merited, not what was lost. (21:29)

Margin Notes from The **Second** Book of **Kings**:

385. Sometimes the Lord's blessings come by simple means. (5:13,14)
386. Sometimes, when we seek things unrighteously or seek the wrong things, we find that having them brings us more trouble and may make our life situation more intolerable. (5:22-27)
387. Just as faithfulness blesses us, faithlessness will destroy us. (7:18,19)

Margin Notes from The **First** Book of **Chronicles**:

388. The choice to sin is the choice to suffer. (9:1)

Margin Notes from The **Second** Book of **Chronicles**:

389. Following a poor council, which answers to a lust for prestige and power, results in loss and personal destruction. (10:13-19)
390. Those who rebel against God lose His protection and blessings. (25:14-16)
391. When taught properly in childhood, it is possible, and perhaps more likely, to return to righteousness, even if great sin is committed. (33:11-13)

Margin Notes from **Ezra**:

392. The Recipe for True and Meaningful Success—Trust the Lord Rather Than Man. (8:22)
393. Through His mercy, God gives us more than we "deserve." (9:13)

Margin Notes from The Book of **Nehemiah**:

394. Remember! Your family is a gift and a blessing to you. You are expected to love them, to teach them the laws of God, and to defend them from all threats to their well-being. (4:14)

Margin Notes from The Book of **Esther**:

395. When we are sincerely faithful and humble, Heavenly Father will raise us up to noble and great works and stations. (8:1,2)

Margin Notes from The Book of **Job**:

396. Satan can tempt; he can cause sufferings, but he cannot take life from the living. (1:12)

397. Some of our trials are the result of our own choices. Some of them are the result of the choices of others. Some are the effects of Satan's assaults against us. Some are simply the consequences of this imperfect mortal life. How much Heavenly Father enables, how much He allows, and how much He averts, we do not know, but what we do know is this. He will never permit more than we can endure and overcome and He will turn all of our trials to our good and benefit IF we will let Him, by believing, trusting, and relying upon Him! (2:1-6)

398. Too many people show faith when life is good but lose it when rough times come. (2:10)

399. Too often unwarranted reproof is administered by those who believe only what they want to

believe despite the truth that is placed before them. (15:2-9)

400. When faith is not lost through trials, testimony is increased. (42:5,6)

Margin Notes from The Book of **Psalms**:

401. With the Lord as our guide, the path is clear, and as we follow it, we are richly blessed. (23)

402. Unless we stand with the Lord, we cannot stand against Satan. (28:1)

403. You are the author of your own story, but remember, it is God who is the author of all things good, in this world and in your life. (100)

404. No amount of perseverance and persuasion justifies disobedience in any way. (106:32,33)

405. Do not put your trust in man, for Heavenly Father is your only sure source of victory. (108:12,13)

406. Knowledge and wisdom of true and eternal worth comes through the Lord's gospel, not through the means of man. (119:99,100)

Margin Notes from The **Proverbs**:

407. Focus on the gospel, always—in ALL Ways! (7:2)

408. Loving and devoted parents do not spare the rod of discipline, but they do not wield it with the hand of punishment or cruelty. (13:24)
409. To be successful, work is requisite. We cannot simply plan and talk; we must also do. (14:23)
410. It is adversity that strengthens our faith; that is why we need it. (24:10)
411. Do not take judgment to be yours to mete out. If you do the punishing, you may find that the Lord will let it stand. So, leave judgment to the Lord. (24:16-18)
412. Do not accept or support the wicked in their wickedness. (24:24,25)
413. He who has, is least satisfied. He who has not, is most appreciative. (27:7)

Margin Notes from **Ecclesiastes**:

414. Nothing of this world has value beyond this world. (2:16-19)
415. Things in life, done in the right time and order, bring joy and reward. Done in any other order or time, they may lead to difficulties. (3:1-8)
416. All creatures—not just man—have a purpose for being. (3:17,18)
417. It is of critical importance to become and remain teachable. (4:13)

418. It is essential that we live faithfully, without compromise, because this life is limited, and when we die, we can do no more toward the acquisition of exaltation. (9:5,6)

419. Mortal life is the same for ALL. Here, we work to learn, grow, and receive from God our reward. That which is truly worth receiving cannot be obtained IN this life, but it is won by that which we DO in this life. In the end, we all die, leaving everything temporal behind, going on to that which we earned. (9:11)

420. Take advantage of opportunities when they come, for opportunities not taken may not be had again. (11)

421. Rather than always seeking change or challenging things in your life, accept what you have and make the most of it. (11)

422. By what we are when we die, we shall receive our eternal judgment. (11:3)

423. There is eternal meaning to life, but only through God and the keeping of His commandments. (12)

424. We know that we lived before we were born and we will live after we die because we cannot return to where we have not been. (12:7)

425. Put God first, and everything else will fall into place. (12:13)

Margin Notes from The Book of the Prophet **Isaiah**:

426. The repentant are forgiven; the obedient are blessed; the wicked are destroyed. (1:18-20)
427. We radiate what we are. (3:9)
428. Our rewards are determined by our choices. (3:9)
429. To justify themselves, sinners deny the truth and make excuses for their sins. (5:20)
430. The gospel of Jesus Christ has been, is being, and will be taught to everyone who ever has lived, lives now, or will live on this earth, that all may be made justifiably accountable. (6:9,10)
431. Those who trust in God will be protected; those who do not, will not. (8:13,14)
432. Even in the midst of the sorest trials or deepest sins, true repentance is possible. (9:12)
433. The Savior never abandons us; if we are alone, we have abandoned Him. (9:17)
434. Though we may not realize it, the Lord often carries out His plan for us through other people. (10:7)
435. Righteous men are as rare and precious and priceless gems. (13:12)
436. Internal strife is more destructive to a nation, a church, a family, and individual, etc., than is any enemy. (19:2)

437. No matter how great the power of man is, God's power always has, does still, and always will exceed it. (31:3)

438. Do yourself a favor: keep the commandments, speak the truth, work righteousness, maintain purity in thought, words, and actions, be fair and just, never take advantage of others, and do not find fault; instead, look for the good in ALL. (33:15)

439. Christ brings peace, but He also brings judgments upon the wicked. (45:7)

Margin Notes from The Book of the Prophet **Jeremiah**:

440. Too often we hear too many people fault God for the struggles in their lives and choose to turn away from Him. One may ask, "What fault could God really have?" There is only one answer to that question, "NONE!!" (2:5)

441. When people are walking the path of unrighteous-ness, the Lord, though He will not walk with them, He works with them, to bring them back to the path of righteousness for as long as there is a chance, even the smallest hope, that they will follow Him. If, however, they reach the point of no return, He lets them reap what they have sown. (14:11,12)

442. Mankind—on an individual basis—receive from God what they have earned through obedience or disobedience. (16:10-12)
443. Whereas children are affected by what their parents are and do, they are not punished for the sins of their parents. (31:29,30)
444. The Lord requires that we honor our covenants and keep our promises. They are not to be given in vain nor taken lightly. Broken covenants bring condemnation. (34:8,9,11,17)
445. The Lord's will, no matter how it appears to us, is always the best for us. (42:6)

Margin Notes from The **Lamentations** of Jeremiah:

446. To neglect the needs of one's children is a grievous sin! (2:11-13 & 4:3-6)

Margin Notes from The Book of the Prophet **Ezekiel**:

447. God strengthens us, making us equal to our tasks, when we do His will. (3:8)
448. When doing the Lord's work, we must speak His words, not our own. (3:26,27)

449. Doing things in secret, suggests an awareness that what you are doing is wrong. So, you should not be doing it. (8:7-12)

450. The wicked do not look for, listen to, or recognize the truth. (12:2)

451. False prophecies and personal choices made without consideration of truth, are like mortar made without lime. Such mortar cannot stand up to the weather. Such prophecies and choices do not hold fast against challenges, trials, or persecutions. (13:10-12)

452. Personal interpretations and opinions that are uninspired can lead people astray and keep them from seeking or finding the truth. (13:17-22)

453. You are judged according to your own thoughts, words, and actions, not by those of anyone else. (18:5-9)

454. Former righteousness cannot save those who turn to wickedness. We all must continue in righteousness—doing that which is good—throughout the whole of our lives. (18:10-17)

455. We get what we give. We receive what we earn. (22:31)

456. Righteous deeds do not cancel out works of iniquity. To exact forgiveness, repentance must be complete and sincere. (33:12,13)

457. Daily transgression with daily insincere or incomplete repentance is not pleasing to God. For repentance to be acceptable is must be accompanied by restitution, and forsaking of the sin. (33:14-19)

Margin Notes from The Book of **Daniel**:

458. Those who are loyal to God and true to their faith, who do not falter, even in the face of painful persecution, are protected and greatly blessed by God. (3:8-29)

459. The Lord will send messengers when we humbly seek knowledge. Of course, the Adversary will try to stop them. That is when the Mighty are sent to assist the Angels. (10:12-14)

Margin Notes from **Hosea**:

460. The Lord wants us to be devoted to the gospel, not merely to worship. (6:6)

461. After judgment, there will be no repentance, because there will be no sin. All will be assigned to a kingdom whose laws they live. (13:14)

Margin Notes from **Joel**:

462. To survive the War, we must train with The Angels. (2:12-14)

Margin Notes from **Amos**:

463. When sin has been committed too many times, or when too many sins have been committed, and repentance is not complete or sincere, the penalty must and will be paid. (1:9-13)

Margin Notes from **Obadiah**:

464. There is no security for the wicked from the justice of the Lord. (1:4)

Margin Notes from **Jonah**:

465. All the children of God are judged according to their knowledge of the gospel teachings, according to their knowledge of right and wrong. (4:11)

Margin Notes from **Micah**:

466. God does not fulfill false prophesies. (3:5,7)

Margin Notes from **Nahum**:

467. God is good, just, and merciful in His dealings with His children. (1:2-11)

Margin Notes from **Habakkuk**:

468. The sinful suffer afflictions because of their wrong choices. But why, when we seek to do what is right and be the best that we can be, we still suffer trials and tribulations? Because The Lord tests the faithfulness of righteousness! (1:12,13)

Margin Notes from **Zephaniah**:

469. The humble and righteous are assured of protection and blessings as they continue to honor and obey the Lord. (2:3)

Margin Notes from **Haggai**:

470. We are to look closely at our lives and make all necessary changes to bring us closer to the Lord. (1:5-8)

Margin Notes from **Zechariah**:

471. Those who refuse to hear and obey the word of the Lord condemn themselves to the consequences of their own choices. (7:9,10)

Margin Notes from **Malachi**:

472. The Lord rewards our righteousness through both temporal and spiritual blessings. (3:10,11)

BIBLE-NEW TESTAMENT

Margin Notes from The Gospel According to
St. **Matthew**:

473. We are judged, not only for our actions, but for our influence as well. (5:19)

474. Remove yourself from any person, place, thing, idea, concept, teaching, or activity—anything—that leads you away from God and His Gospel. (5:29,30 & 18:8,9)

475. When talking personally with Heavenly Father, we must remember to pray privately and sincerely, making our prayers a true conversation, not merely the recitation of the same phrases. (6:7,8)

476. The Treasures of Heaven are godly attributes, correct knowledge, enduring faith, righteous judgment, equitable justice, divine mercy and eternal truth. (6:19-21)

477. The person who is actively devoted to God is filled with goodness and light.

478. The person who is not devoted to God is full of darkness and sin. (6:22,23)

479. Restrict your choices to that which is wholesome and righteous. (7:13,14)

480. As you learn the truth, live the truth. As you live the truth, teach the truth, both through words and example. (10:27)

481. We cannot say one thing and do another and remain committed to God and His gospel. (12:25)

482. Between black and white, there is no grey. It is only when we mix them that their appearance changes. So it is, with good and bad, truth and error, right and wrong. (12:30)

483. Words, actions, attitudes, and ideals are all determined by the intentions of the character. (12:33-37)

484. Without faith, it is not possible to see the Signs from Heaven, hear the Still Small Voice, or feel the Touch of the Spirit. (12:39)

485. If we do not actively continue to increase and strengthen our testimony of the truth—the Lord's gospel—we will lose it. (13:12)

486. Those who know you best and are closest to you are often the least likely to be taught by you or follow your example. (13:57)

487. As we wade through The Sea of Life—our trials, troubles, and challenges—let us remember the example of Peter.

488. He walked on the water when he had faith; we can "walk on the water" through faith. He sank when he doubted; we "sink" when we question the truth or surrender our faith to faction.

489. He was saved when he called out to Jesus, and reached up for His hand ~ we can be saved when we "call or 'text'" Jesus and take His hand." (14:28-33)

490. To be a Little Child is to be humble, obedient to the Gospel, submissive to God, kind, and forgiving. (18:1-6)

491. When a person goes astray, we are to go and find him or her.

492. When that person returns, repents, and lives according to the gospel, there is great joy and happiness felt by those who love him or her.

493. But let us always remember, as a help to keep us from going astray and to encourage us to continue to extend the helping, compassionate hand, that one who has strayed is NOT more favored or blessed than those who did not stray.

494. What was lost as a consequence of the wayward journey is not automatically reclaimed upon return. He or she must go on, moving forward from that point. (18:12-14)

495. We receive what we earn by how we live. (20:1-16)

496. Those who are called to lead are called to serve, not to rule. (23:8-12)

497. The outward appearance of obedience and devotion to God, if not coupled with inner truth,

sincerity, and commitment, adds the sin of hypocrisy to those sins already committed. (23:13-36)

498. Heavenly Father does not expect more of us than that which we can do, but He does expect us to use our knowledge and abilities to help and serve others, not just ourselves. Then, consequential to our choice of action, rewards and blessings are equivalent to our intent and performance. (25:14-30)

499. We must never let ourselves be so sure of our commitment to the gospel that we fail to be ever mindful in our living of it. (26:31-35)

500. Rather than seeking to avoid struggle, we must seek the Lord's help to journey through the struggle so that we can learn and grow from it. (26:42)

501. Our responsibilities and accountabilities can never be rightfully transferred to anyone else. (27:24,25)

Margin Notes from The Gospel According to St. **Mark**:

502. Those who are great in the Kingdom of God are those who are like little children here. (9:37)

503. Sacrifice with a devout intent in giving is the greater gift than that which is given.

504. (12:41-44)

Margin Notes from The Gospel According to St. **Luke**:

505. Too often people do not see the value in, or give respect to the people who are familiar to them. Nor do they accept instruction, even of the truth, from them. (4:16-24)
506. The unrighteousness finds fault with everything they do not want to accept. (7:33-35)
507. The greater the sin committed, the greater the repentance that is required. (7:41-43)
508. Those who have the gospel are expected to share it with others both through teaching and by example. (8:16-18)
509. To be worthy of exaltation, we must be loyal to Christ and His gospel over and above everything else. (9:23-27)
510. A person is either committed to the Lord or he is not; there is no in between. (11:17)
511. What you work for, you love and what you love, you work for. So, make sure that what you love and work for, is that which is eternally worth having. (12:34)
512. Be humble and you will earn honor. Be prideful and you will earn shame. (14:8-11)

513. The nature of the individual is generally constant across experiences.

514. He who is irresponsible or sinful in some things will be likewise in other things.

515. He who does not make the right choices regarding others will do no better for himself.

516. We cannot live the gospel and love God, while sinning and pleasing man, for anything that is not aligned with the truth is of the devil and opposed to God.

517. If we prove to be careless with one thing, we will inevitably be careless with another. Therefore, we cannot live just some of God's Laws.

518. We live it ALL, or it is as good as not living it at all. (16:10-13)

519. Empirical evidence does not convince one of the Truth. It is Faith that grows and sustains recognition of true truths. Without it, there can be no real testimony. (24:18-24)

Margin Notes from The Gospel According to St. **John**:

520. To return to sin after repentance brings greater sorrow and suffering. (5:14)

521. Those who sincerely live their lives aligned with the Gospel are free from the dictatorship of the adversary. (8:31,32)
522. Do the things the Lord did: love, teach, serve. (13:13-15)
523. Christ is our example in all things. We must be like Him. When we strive to be so, in our association with others, through the love of Christ, we will seek for their best good, not just to please them. (13:27-29)

Margin Notes from **Acts** of the Apostles:

524. Miracles are available to those of faith who seek them. However, only the truly faithful recognize them when they come. (3:12,13)
525. Lying is damnable, and as with every other sin or transgression, an accomplice is as accountable as the perpetrator. (5:1-10)
526. Obedience to God is preeminent over obedience to man. (5:29)
527. The work of God cannot be stopped by man. (5:38,39)
528. The power of God is far greater than that of the Adversary. (8:9-13)
529. To receive the Spirit and blessings, the right things must be done for the right reasons. (8:21)
530. Do Not Challenge God!! (11:18)

531. For the honest in heart, even negative examples can have a positive influence, because they will know how to properly respond to them and learn from them. (19:13-20)
532. Sometimes, those who oppose truth do so either because of their love of worldly things or their fear of material loss. (19:24-28)

Margin Notes from The Epistle of Paul the Apostle to the **Romans**:

533. The Gospel of the Lord is the only transportation—The Train, to the only worthwhile destination—Eternal Life, and Faith is the fuel that powers it. (1:16,17)
534. Those who are prideful change the truth to suit their desires. (1:21-25)
535. We are not qualified to judge others. (2:1,2)
536. Righteousness is more than just good works; it is faith combined with action. (4:4,5)
537. Through faith, through trials, and through faith exercised threw trials, we are spiritually strengthened. (5:1-5)
538. You cannot serve yourself and the Lord. Seeking worldly pleasures alienates you from God. (8:5,6)
539. Faith yields patience, which yields growth. (8:24,25)

540. Nothing and no one, including the adversary, can pull us away from God; we would have to choose to let go of His hand. Nothing but our own choices can ever defeat us. (8:35-39)
541. We are to respect others "where they are." We are not to judge them; we are to help them. (14:1-3,11-13)

Margin Notes from The **First** Epistle of Paul the Apostle to The **Corinthians**:

542. Missionary efforts must teach to the spirit, not to the mind. (2:4,5)
543. We learn the wisdom of the world through intellectual study and academic learning. We learn the wisdom of God through scriptural study and prayerful learning by the Spirit. (2:9-11)
544. We receive what we are ready for, as we are ready for it. (3:2)
545. We receive what we achieve. (3:8)
546. As we are tested, our work is too. (3:13-17)
547. Only God has knowledge enough to judge us. We do not, so we must not. (4:5)
548. We are to cleanse ourselves of sin by replacing inappropriate, unacceptable behaviors and thoughts with those that are Christlike. We are

also to remove ourselves from the company of those who would lead us astray. (5:7,8)

549. We are responsible and accountable for the example we set and the influence we wield. (8:10-13)

550. We get what we earn. (9:10)

551. Teach others eternal knowledge on their level, but do not ever live beneath your own level of spiritual knowledge. (9:22,23)

552. We cannot be tempted beyond our ability to refuse the temptation. (10:12,13)

553. We cannot cavort with the world and still have the spirit with us. (10:21)

554. We can associate with people of the world, but in doing so, we must not do anything that would violate the gospel or offend God. We must conduct ourselves in a manner that will testify of God accurately and not be deliberately offensive to anyone! (10:31,32)

555. Let only those who follow Christ be your exemplar. (11:1)

556. How the Lord's word is extended and His work is accomplished may vary, but the word and work, themselves do not. (12:4-6)

557. We are to care for others as we would care for ourselves, and we are to care for ourselves as God would have us do. (12:25,26)

Margin Notes from The **Second** Epistle of Paul the Apostle to The **Corinthians**:

558. No trial is too devastating for those who accept and live the gospel, and rely upon Christ for help when the trial becomes more than they can endure. (4:8,9)

559. We are to share our resources with those in need, so that all can live adequately. (8:11-15)

560. We are blessed with the same measure with which we bless. (9:6,7)

561. The Lord's praise is the only praise of true value. (10:17,18)

562. For us to grow spiritually, not only must we overcome trials, but we also must withstand corrections. (12:7-10)

563. The closer we become to the Lord, the more like Him we become, the more the world will reject us, and that is good!! (14:15)

Margin Notes from The Epistle of Paul the Apostle to The **Galatians**:

564. In times of need, when all that can be done is done, we are to help and support one another, but in all things, we are to do all we can do for ourselves before we depend upon the mercy of others. (6:2-5)

Margin Notes from The Epistle of Paul the Apostle to The **Ephesians**:

565. We cannot, on our own, do everything for ourselves that is required to be saved from the Adversary's thwarts. We need the Savior's help. (2:8,9)

Margin Notes from The Epistle of Paul the Apostle to The **Philippians**:

566. Do not openly sorrow; you may bring greater suffering to yourself. Instead, employ your smile and rely upon God. (4:6,7)

Margin Notes from The Epistle of Paul the Apostle to The **Colossians**:

567. We must strive to deal with others as the Lord deals with us—lovingly, mercifully, justly. (4:1,2,5,6)

Margin Notes from The **First** Epistle of Paul the Apostle to The **Thessalonians**:

568. To help ourselves be prepared for the Lord's return, along with aligning our lives with the

gospel, we must seek to improve our relationships with others and with God. (5:8-22)

Margin Notes from The **Second** Epistle of Paul the Apostle to The **Thessalonians**:

569. Be careful not to enmesh yourself with the wayward, but do not forsake them either. Instead, help them return to the Lord. (3:14-16)

Margin Notes from The **First** Epistle of Paul the Apostle to **Timothy**:

570. Do take care of your body, but give more heed to your spirit. (4:7,8)
571. Those who seek wealth for their own profit, rather than for the purpose of doing the Lord's work, inevitably fall away from God. (6:8-12)

Margin Notes from The **Second** Epistle of Paul the Apostle to **Timothy**:

572. Faith in Christ is rewarded in kind. (2:11-13)
573. Study and share the Lord's gospel, but do not debate it, and do not mix it with the philosophies of man. (2:14-17)

574. Satan wars with the greatest fervor against those who are most righteous because, through their righteousness, they are his most powerful enemies. (3:12)
575. The textbooks for discipleship are the Scriptures. (3:16,17)

Margin Notes from The Epistle of Paul the Apostle to **Titus**:

576. The pure in heart are pure in heart because they shield their heart from impurity. (1:15,16)

Margin Notes from The Epistle of Paul the Apostle to **Philemon**:

577. Through the gospel, we become family with all who come to the gospel. (1:15)

Margin Notes from The Epistle of Paul the Apostle to **Hebrews**:

578. Because Jesus suffered all things, He can comfort us in all things. (2:18)
579. Those who have received the Lord's gospel, but are weak in the learning and living of it, are not

able to teach with the power with which those who are strong and obedient. (5:12-14)

580. We must be obedient, steadfast, and immovable in living gospel law, for once blessings are lost, they are lost. (12:11-15)

581. Want what you have and be grateful for it. (13:5,6)

The General Epistle of **James**:

582. We grow through trials and faced well. (1:2-4)

583. To gain the blessings that can come through trials, we must journey through those trials with faith. (1:5-7)

584. We either have faith, or we do not! (1:8)

585. All people are equal in the sight of God and they must be equal in ours as well. (2:1-8)

586. If we transgress one law, we lose the blessings of them all. (2:9,10)

587. For faith to be empowered, we must express it through works—devotion, obedience to God, and service to others. (2:17,18,20,22,24,26)

588. In any situation or circumstance, we must first do all that we can do! (2:14-26)

589. By unkind words, great harms are perpetrated. (3:5)

590. We cannot speak both lovingly and hatefully at
the same time; only the bitter will be conveyed.
(3:10-12)
591. The gospel is not cultural. There is one truth for
everyone. (3:17)
592. Prayers for the wrong things cannot be
answered. (4:3)
593. The wealthy who have lived selfishly shall lose
everything. (5:1-5)

The **First** Epistle General of **Peter**:

594. Wives are to honor their husband's
stewardship, through which they preside, not to
rule. Husbands are to honor and care for their
wives as they work together as one. (3:1,2,7)
595. The beauty of a woman is a gentle spirit. (3:3,4)

The **Second** Epistle General of **Peter**:

596. The greater the knowledge that is possessed,
the greater the fall and punishment are for
those who choose rebellion. (2:20-22)

The **First** Epistle General of **John**:

597. We are hypocrites if or when we say we love God
and then do not live His gospel.

(1:1-10)

598. That which is bad is bad; what is good is good. (3:6-8)

599. Love must be demonstrated through action. (3:18)

The **Second** Epistle of **John**:

600. To avoid deception, we must avoid close association with the wiles of the world. (1:10,11)

The **Third** Epistle of **John**:

601. There is no compromise: we are either following God or we are following Satan. (1:11)

The General Epistle of **Jude**:

602. We must adhere to the gospel and help others do the same. (1:20-23)

The **Revelation** of St. John the Divine:

603. Temporal wealth does not make you rich; Spiritual wealth does. (3:17-19)

604. Be Prepared!! Live every day as if it were your last day, for no one knows the exact day that the Savior will return. Nor do we know the day

that will be our finale, whether it be before, at
the time of, or after the Savior's Second
Coming. (16:15)

THE BOOK OF MORMON

The **First** Book of **Nephi**:

605. There will be times when we must be willing to make sacrifices in order to obey the Lord. (2:4)

606. Show gratitude; see the blessings, even in adversity. (2:6)

607. We are blessed when we obey graciously. (3:6)

608. Heavenly Father does not ask us to do what cannot be done. (3:7)

609. When we fail to obey the directives of God, we will be left to the natural consequences of our choices. (3:18)

610. Signs and miracles do not result in faith. Faith results in signs and miracles. (3:29-31)

611. We must know the gospel in order to live the gospel; so study the gospel and teach the gospel. (4:14,15)

612. An oath is a sacred trusted vow; it was then; it is now. (4:32-37)

613. To attune with the Spirit, we must take time, in quietude, to ponder, and to listen. (11:1)

614. When one does not live worthily, the Lord's blessings fall to another who does. (13:41,42)

615. We are judged by our thoughts, words, and actions ~ those made apparent and those hidden. (15:32,33)

616. The blessings of God are sometimes bestowed upon us through miraculous means, but they are often bestowed through everyday means, as well. (16:29)

617. Sometimes we fail to see what we need to see because we expect to see something else. (17:41)

618. The Lord will teach us all things, but we must go to Him in prayer and we must go often. (18:3)

619. There is a purpose in every trial. (18:11)

The **Second** Book of **Nephi**:

620. Without opposition in all things, there would be nothing. (2:11-13)

621. We need opposition in order to exercise agency. (2:16)

622. We can receive what we ask of the Lord when we ask for the right things. (4:35)

623. Neither Heavenly Father nor Jesus ever chooses to abandon or ignore us. It is man's choice to sin that creates the divide, if there is one. (7:1)

624. In the end, as we become, we shall be. (9:16)

625. We are to use what we have to do God's work, not to increase worldly possessions. (9:51)

626. When a man puts more value on his accomplishments than on the gospel, he has made idols. (12:8)
627. We cannot rightfully credit ourselves alone for what the Lord helps us do. (20:15)
628. Acceptance of the gospel is the beginning—living it and enduring must follow. (31:20)
629. If we do not understand, it is because we do not seek to know. (32:4,5)

The Book of **Jacob**:

630. Love of the server from the served follows service. (1:10)
631. Riches are for doing the Lord's work. (2:18,19)
632. The importance of family—expressed through love, devotion, and active relations—is paramount in the gospel of the Lord. ((3:7)
633. The Lord's will is always the best course of action. (4:9,10)
634. Looking beyond the mark causes us to fall. (4:14)

The Book of **Enos**:

635. It is through personal struggle within ourselves that we are enabled to overcome our personal nemeses. (1:1,4)

636. Praying in faith is more than just believing you
will be heard and answered; it is praying for the
right things. (1:15)

The Book of **Jarom**:

637. Live each day the way you would live it if Jesus
were here with you. (1:11)

The Book of **Omni**:

638. A Key for Discernment—If it is from God, it is
good. If it is from Satan, it is bad. (1:25)

The **Words of Mormon**:

639. Lead by example: do what you would expect to
have done. (1:13)

The Book of **Mosiah**:

640. The most effective leaders work with their
people; they do not just command them. (2:14)
641. Service is one of the greatest acts of love. (2:17)
642. Despite all that Heavenly Father does for us—
even the sustaining of our lives—all He asks of
us is obedience. Ergo, despite all the good

prayers of gratitude we can offer, we could never express adequate thanks. (2:20-22)

643. Sinners require repentance. The innocent are covered by the Atonement. (3:12,18)

644. Guilt causes discomfort in the face of righteousness, whereas innocence provides peace and assurance. (3:25)

645. The carnal man is less than dust because dust obeys God, he does not. (4:2)

646. We must help others just because they need help, always remembering that all of us receive help from God. (4:16-19)

647. As the Lord gives to us, we must give to others. (4:21)

648. God asks all of us to serve and to give what we can to others in times of need. Even the poor are required to give what they can, even if it is only through the spirit of sincere desire. (4:24,25)

649. Be Careful! Guard yourself and sin not, for all sins, "big" and "small," are destructive. (4:29,30)

650. Without trust in, belief in, knowledge of, and dependence upon God, we are left to our own inadequate abilities. (10:10,11)

651. The Lord cannot help or bless the unrepentant because He does not reward sin. (11:20-25)

652. Often, we bring about what happens to us by what we do or do not do for others. (13:9,10)

653. In the eyes of the Lord, all mankind is equal, and so they must be in our eyes too. (23:7)

654. Patience is required for faith to grow. (23:21,22)

655. To truly know Christ, we must be like Christ. (26:24)

656. True conversion to the gospel of Jesus Christ brings sincere brotherly love for all. (28:3)

The Book of **Alma:**

657. The Lord strengthens the righteous, making the impossible, possible. (2:27-31)

658. Sin brings its own punishment. (3:19)

659. By our works, we demonstrate whom we serve ~ the Savior or Satan. (5:38,39)

660. God does not break His own laws; so neither can we. (7:20,21)

661. When life meets its end and resurrection opens the next door, the body will be perfected and the memory will be complete; our minds forget nothing; everything is stored. (11:43)

662. It is foolish to try to play hide-and-seek with God because nothing can be hidden from Him. (12:3)

663. We receive knowledge according to our devotions to the living of it. (12:9,10)

664. Repentance is the prerequisite for blessings. So, do it now! (13:20-30)

665. The righteous may, at the time, suffer, making the judgments against the wicked justified. (14:11)

666. Physical illness, mental and emotional illness can spring from spiritual illness. Is that not all the more reason to strengthen and fortify one's spirituality? (15:3)

667. Greed leads to wickedness, but laziness and inordinate dependence also lead to spiritual stagnation. (17:14)

668. When the Lord opens the door, walk in!! (18:21-23)

669. We keep our faith. Heavenly Father keeps His promises. (19:23)

670. The gentle but firm, soft and loving approach is more persuasive than any amount of might. (20:21-27)

671. On our own, there is a limit to what we can do; with God's help, there is nothing we cannot do. (26:11,12)

672. Deceivers have no evidence to support their claims, but truth does. Therefore, truth has the power to confound error. (30:40,41)

673. It is more blessed to humble oneself than it is to be humbled! (32:13-15)

674. Plant and nourish the gospel seed, that is the Word of God, remembering that for a seed to grow, it must be planted in good soil and

adequately nourished aright. Then its fruits can be reaped. (32:27-43)

675. On the day of judgment, we will find that we are our own judges, in that it is by our works here that our judgment will be decided there. (41:3)

676. The prideful and the unbelieving cannot see the hand of the Lord in their life or the lives of any others. (44:9)

677. Faith plus obedience equals blessings. (48:20)

678. Faith without doubt equals power. (56:47)

679. The law must be lived as it is written. (57:21)

680. To receive God's help, we must first do our part and continue to do so. (60:11)

681. Trials that come upon us because of the choices, words, and actions of others stand as witnesses against them, if they do not properly and completely repent. (60:13,14)

682. The most powerful enemy of nations, states, towns, churches, organizations, families, and individuals is contention and conflict from within! (60:16)

683. First, we must cleanse ourselves from sin, faults, and weaknesses. Then we are prepared to order our lives and help others. (60:23)

684. Freedom does not mean that everyone can have and do as they please without having to pay the price of consequences. (62:9,10)

The Book of **Helaman:**

685. Hardships may be for the purpose of humbling. (11:4,7,15)

686. We are judged according to both our degree of knowledge and our depth of repentance. (14:18,19)

The **Third** Book of **Nephi:**

687. The Recipe for Righteousness: Repent and Forsake Sin, Obey God's Commandments, Diligently Serve the Lord. (5:3)

688. Contention is not of God; in fact, it puts us at odds with Him. To be in harmony with God, we must be in harmony with His teachings. (11:28-30)

689. Faith is more powerful than fact. (12:2)

690. We seek after that which we love. (13:21)

691. Follow Christ's example: put the needs and righteous desires of people before "schedules." (17:5,6)

The **Fourth** Book of **Nephi:**

692. Prosperity is wrought through obedience. (1:5,7,10)

The Book of **Mormon**:

693. For the act of repenting to be an expression of
true repentance it must be motivated by Godly
sorrow, sincere remorse for the wrongs
committed—not worldly sorrow—grief for
oneself, for what was lost to them. (2:10-15)

694. Despite the influences that abound around us,
we are perfectly capable of choosing to learn
and to do that which is right and good in the
sight of God. (2:18,19)

695. Heavenly Father gives us all the opportunities
and help He can to enable us to return to Him.
(3:3)

696. Prayers are answered; miracles still happen.
(9:20,21)

The Book of **Ether**:

697. Even when faith is demonstrated, answers
may not come quickly. (1:43)

698. True faith, exercised unwaveringly, leads to
sure knowledge. (3:19,20)

699. Philanthropy cannot atone for immorality.
(10:11)

700. There is a point of no return. (15:19)

The Book of **Moroni**:

701. Do good for the right reasons, or it is wrong. (7:11)
702. Properly seek that which is right and you will receive it. (7:26,29)
703. Once you have been blessed with the Word of God, share it! Teach it to all, even if they will not hear. (9:6)
704. Faith plus Hope plus Charity—working together—equals Righteousness. (10:20-22)

THE DOCTRINE AND COVENANTS

705. There is no shame in being among the weak of the world, for they are those who, though they may lack in the power of the world, they are humble and mighty before the Lord. (1:19)

706. Heavenly Father grants what is earned. (1:35,36)

707. God's work cannot be stopped. Man's work can be thwarted. (3:1-4)

708. Trust in God. Do not put man above Him. (3:7,8)

709. What does Heavenly Father expect of us? Truth unfeigned, nothing less!! (5:4)

710. What does Heavenly Father want from us? Total commitment, nothing less!! (5:21)

711. Blessings and protection come through humble obedience. (5:28,30-35)

712. Personal revelation is ours for the asking, when we obey the Law of the Lord. (6:5-8)

713. Do good and fear not. (6:33,36)

714. Revelation and knowledge do come through faith but they must be sought. (8:1,2,10)

715. To receive what we seek we must seek after the right things. Afterall, Heavenly Father seeks to help us, not hinder us. (8:10)

716. There is no justifiable excuse for sin. (10:28)

717. To receive what we seek, we must seek what is right and obey the commandments of God. (11:5-8)

718. First Priority, seek after things eternal, not things temporal. (11:12-14)

719. Christlike traits qualify and enable us to do the Lord's work. (12:6,8)

720. Look to the scriptures for guidance and knowledge. (18:3,4)

721. Knowledge of truth is available to those who seek it in faith. (18:17-19)

722. We receive what we are ready to bear. (19:21,22)

723. We will not have to stand alone at the judgement bar of God because Jesus advocates for us. (29:5-7)

724. What we receive from Heavenly Father and the works He entrusts to us are predicated upon our obedience to His laws and our willingness to do His will. (39:9-11)

725. There will be many who will not be prepared for the Savior's return because they will choose to believe it is still far off, not in their life-time. (45:2)

726. For those who choose to accept Him as the Father's Emissary, and live their lives aligned with His Law, Jesus will be their Defense Attorney. (45:3-5)

727. Gifts of the Spirit are for growth and protection. (46:8.9)
728. Be it right or wrong, too many people choose to believe that which is comfortable to them. (49:2)
729. We must be purified, cleansed through repentance, to receive what we seek and we must seek for that which is right, that which Heavenly Father wants us to have. (50:28-30)
730. Focus on the ways and works of God, not of man. (53:2)
731. Violating a covenant made is a more serious transgression than never having made the covenant. (54:4,5)
732. We are to do all that we can do for ourselves and not just expect others to provide for us. We are also expected to help others, and not live in excess. (56:13,16,17)
733. There is divine purpose in earthly suffering. (58:3,4)
734. Talents are to be used for good works. (60:2,3)
735. Signs follow the exercise of faith; they are not to be sought. (63:7-11)
736. Idleness is a sin. (68:30,31)
737. To "fear" God is to respect Him. To serve God is to be obedient and to do His work. (76:5)
738. Meditation, that is spiritual pondering, opens the Windows of Heaven. (76:19)

739. We are required to live up to all the knowledge we have. (82:3)

740. No one can ever claim to not know right from wrong; we all do. It is called conscience. (84:46)

741. Responsibility to share the gospel rests with everyone who has it. (84:76)

742. Just because they can, the strong should always help the weak. (84:106)

743. Truth is eternal and from God; anything else is wrong and from Satan. (93:24,25)

744. Deserved chastisement, administered lovingly, is a benefit to us. (95:1)

745. Trials are oft times the soap used to wash away wickedness. (101:2,4,5)

746. Do not live for the love of this life; live to please God. (101:36-38)

747. Preparation is vital to success. (101:72)

748. Those who keep their covenants are greatly blessed. Those who break their covenants are sorely cursed. (104:2,3)

749. Those who could assist but willfully withhold their help from the poor will reap a vat of sour grapes. (104:18)

750. It is important that we serve, but what is more important than the service we render is why we render it. (117:11)

751. Those who persecute righteousness are those who sin against it or deny it. (121:16-21)

752. Struggles faced in this life are like the rungs on a ladder, they enable us to ascend to greater heights. (122:7)
753. Temporal things are temporary. (132:13,14)
754. Purity is requisite to withstand glory. (136:37)

THE PEARL OF GREAT PRICE

Selections from the Book of **Moses:**

755. Satan cannot have power over us unless we let him. (1:16,18,19)
756. Obedience to the Laws of God does not require understanding. If He says, "Do it," just do it. (5:5)

The Book of **Abraham:**

757. Those committed to God continually seek more eternal knowledge. (1:2)
758. Greatness is measured by closeness to God. (3:16)
759. Our performance in our First Estate determined much of what we received in this, our Second Estate. Our performance in this, our Second Estate will determine what we receive for our Eternal State. (3:26)

Joseph Smith – Matthew:

760. Those who accept the Gospel of Christ, continually learn it more and live it well, will not be deceived by falsities. (1:22)
761. Live every day to the full measure of your abilities for no one knows the time of The End, be it theirs or the world's. (1:40)

Joseph Smith – History:

762. Because they are a threat to him, the adversary seeks to destroy those who work for God. (1:20)
763. Heavenly Father employs the humble to do His work. (1:22)
764. Do not deny what the Lord has revealed! You will regret it. (1:25)

ABOUT THE AUTHOR

Eileen DiStasio-Clark is the second oldest of four children. She is the mother of eleven children and grandmother to twenty-three grandchildren, to date. As a member of The Church of Jesus Christ of Latter-Day Saints, she serves in various positions, teaching, leading, and ministering to children, youth, and adults. Currently, she is also a Family History Missionary. Eileen established the Pursuit of Excellence Institute of Family Education, a non-profit organization focused on strengthening the family. Presently she holds an A.A., a B.A., and an M.A. in Clinical Psychology and is working on the completion of her Doctoral Degree.

www.ingramcontent.com/pod-product-compliance
Lightning Source LLC
Chambersburg PA
CBHW040152160726

48006CB00014B/1715

The Writing On The Wall

Eileen DiStasio-Clark

is the second oldest of 4 children. She is the mother of 11 children and grandmother to 23 grandchildren ~ to date. As a member of The Church of Jesus Christ of Latter-Day Saints, she serves in various positions, teaching, leading, and ministering to children, youth, and adults. Currently, she is also a Family History Missionary. Eileen established the Pursuit of Excellence Institute of Family Education, a non-profit organization focused on strengthening the family. Presently she holds an AA, a BA, and an MA in Clinical Psychology and is working on the completion of her Doctoral Degree.

ISBN 979-8-3306-3069-1

90000

9 798330 630691